Draw Dinosaurs!

Lee Duhig

 Mud Puddle inc.
NEW YORK

Draw Dinosaurs

Written & illustrated by
Lee Duhig

©2006 by Mud Puddle, Inc.

Published by
Mud Puddle, Inc.
54 w. 25TH St.
New York, NY 10010

info@mudpuddleinc.com

ISBN: 978-1-60311-031-0

Printed in China

Contents

INTRODUCTION:

Drawing is a fun and rewarding activity that can be enjoyed by all ages and can be done almost anywhere!

This book will show you how to draw the prehistoric animals known as dinosaurs in a few easy-to-follow steps!

You only need a few things to get started. They are:

A pencil with either a B or HB lead
These leads are soft and perfect for drawing.

An inking pen
Make sure the tip is thin so you can ink fine lines.

Colored pencils
Try to get as many colors as you can.

A soft white eraser
You should use this type, since erasers on the end of pencils are usually hard and smudge the pencil lines on the paper.

However, you really only need a pencil to get drawing, so don't worry if you don't have any of the other materials on hand.

How to use this book:

This book is set up in a simple, easy-to-follow way. Here are the steps:

1. We start with a simple squared grid.
Draw some basic body shapes within the grid.

2. Connect the shapes together.

3. Add more shapes to define the subject.

4. Then add details to finish the subject.

5. Finally, ink the figure with a pen. Then color the figure!

The current steps are shown in orange pencil to indicate what you are actively drawing. The previous steps are shown in blue pencil.

Don't feel you have to color the dinosaurs the way they are done in this book. They're just meant to show you one possible way to color them.

No one really knows what color dinosaurs were, so feel free to color them any way you like!

Use your imagination!

Dimetrodon

Not a dinosaur, dimetrodon was actually a pelycosaur, a large, primitive creature that lived millions of years before the dinosaurs. A gigantic carnivore (meat-eater), it had characteristics of mammals and reptiles. Its formidable jaw contained two types of teeth, hence its name, which means "two-measures tooth." Its legs sprawled from its sides, unlike dinosaurs, whose legs were underneath their bodies. The large sail on its back, which is actually a large flap of skin supported by bony spines and is characteristic of pelycosaurs, probably helped to regulate body temperature. Fossils have been found in Texas and Oklahoma.

1. Draw a grid with 4 squares going across and 2 down.

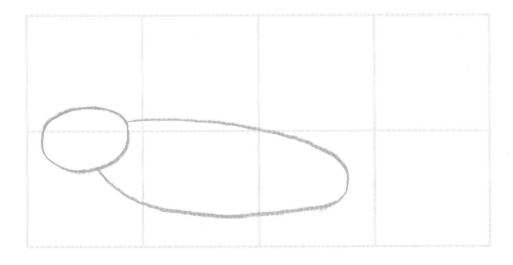

Draw 2 ovals: 1 small oval in the center on the left side of the grid, and another long, stretched oval on the right side of the smaller oval.

2.

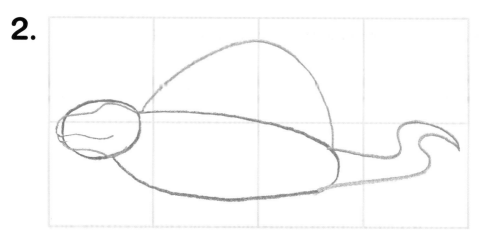

In the small oval, draw in the lines of the head and make the snout extend past the oval.

Next, draw a large, rounded curve above the stretched oval. Then draw some S-shaped curved lines to make the tail.

3.

Draw in the legs of the dino and give it short, pointy toes.

Then, on top of the stretched oval, draw some long, sharp, spines that follow the curved line you drew in step 2.

4. Now you can draw the nostril and eyeball.

To finish the drawing, add rounded "W" shapes on top of the spines that follow the curve above the dino's back.

5. Ink the dino and erase the grid.

Color the body of the dino a BROWNISH GREEN and its belly a TAN color.

Make the webbing between the spines a DARK YELLOW.

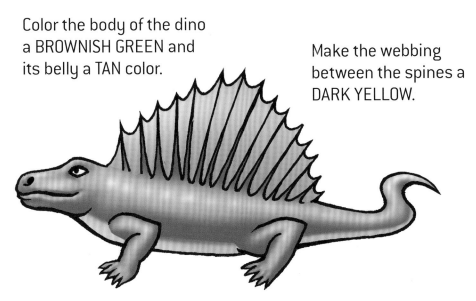

Velociraptor

An extremely fast, two-legged meat-eater with a large brain and 80 very sharp, curved teeth, velociraptor stood about 3 feet (1m) tall. One of the smartest dinosaurs, velociraptor probably hunted in packs that were capable of taking down much larger animals. Dinner was likely to be anything that crossed its path. Its slender legs could sprint up to 40mph (60km/hr). It likely had the ability to jump. Fossils were first discovered in Mongolia in 1924.

1. Draw a grid with 3 squares going across and 3 down.

Draw 2 shapes: an oval shape in the center of the grid, and an "egg" shape in the upper left corner of the grid.

2.

Draw 2 curved lines from the circle to the oval shape.

Add 2 lines curving upward from the right side of the center oval shape to make the tail.

3.

Within the "egg" shape, draw the lines of the head. Add the brow, snout and jaw.

Draw the shape of the arms and the 2 legs of the dino. Give the dino rounded toes and fingers.

4.

Draw the eyeball, nostril, and curve of the mouth.

Add a neck curve line the show the neck twisting.

Draw 3 claws on each hand.

Last, draw 3 claws on the feet, but make the inner claws at least 3 times the size of the other toe claws.

5. Ink your dino and erase the grid.

Color your dino a REDDISH PINK.

Make the eye a BRIGHT YELLOW.

Spinosaurus

This "spiny lizard" is now thought to be the largest land carnivore in history, 50 feet (15m) in length and weighing up to 8 tons. All this weight was carried on two legs, although its two longish "arms" may have allowed it to walk on all fours at times. Fossils were first discovered and named in 1915 in Africa. These were lost in World War II, and it was only a recent discovery of a spinosaurus skull that allowed the creature to take its rightful place in the dinosaur pantheon. Fossils have been found in Northern Africa and Argentina.

1. Draw a grid with 4 squares going across and 3 down.

Draw 2 ovals: 1 large one in the center of the grid and a small one in the upper left corner of the grid.

2.

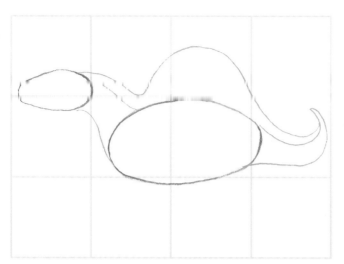

Now draw some curved lines to form the neck and tail.

Above those lines, draw another curved line that follows the neck, arcs up high above the body oval, then sweeps downward into tail lines.

3.

Draw in the shape of the head in the small oval. Give the back of the jaw a triangular point.

Next, draw the arm and leg of the dino.

4.

On the curved line above the neck and body, draw rounded humps and lines to make the spines.

Next, draw in the eye socket, eyeball and a curvy mouth.

Draw curved shapes to separate the claws.

5. Finish by inking the drawing and erasing the grid.

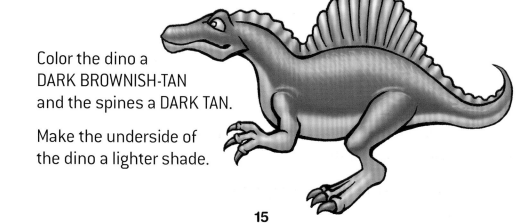

Color the dino a DARK BROWNISH-TAN and the spines a DARK TAN.

Make the underside of the dino a lighter shade.

Tyrannosaurus rex

Perhaps the most famous dinosaur of all, the T-Rex was a huge, fierce, meat-eating predator whose fossils have been found in Mongolia and western North America. This 40 foot (12m)-long creature was up to 20 feet (6m) tall and, like many dinosaurs, walked on its toes! Within its 4 foot (1m)-long jaw were 60 thick teeth that could easily pulverize bone. If its teeth were lost or damaged, T-Rex could grow new ones. Given its tremendous size and weight, the T-Rex was surprisingly agile and fast-moving. T-Rex translates as "tyrant lizard king."

1. Draw a grid with 3 squares going across and 4 down.

Draw 2 ovals: 1 in the middle of the grid, the other toward the upper right corner of the grid.

2.

Draw in 2 curved lines to connect the 2 shapes.

Next, draw the curved lines of the tail on the left side of the center oval.

3.

Define the head shape and add nostrils and eye sockets.

Draw a "wavy" curved line for the lower jaw.

Next, draw the legs and short arms of the dino.

Give the dino 2 hand claws and 3 foot claws.

4.

Draw in a dot for the eye, curved lip lines, and a set of sharp pointy teeth.

Draw two short, vertical lines on the neck to show the neck twisting.

Finally, add the foot claws and foot details. Also, add a 4th claw underneath the right foot.

5. Ink your dino and erase the grid lines.

Color the dino a DARK YELLOW-GREEN.

Stegosaurus

The largest of the "armored dinosaurs," stegosaurus (the name means "covered lizard" or "roof lizard") had a brain about the size of a large nut, which is to say, it wasn't very smart. Two rows of bony plates ran along its back. While their use is unknown, they may have helped regulate the animal's temperature as well as protect the dinosaur against enemies. Stegosaurus was a toothless herbivore (it ate only plants). Fossils were first discovered in Colorado in 1876 and have since been found at sites all over the world.

1. Draw a grid with 4 squares going across and 3 down.

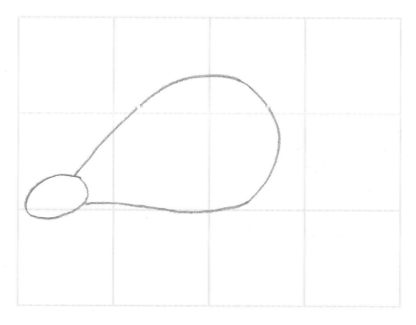

Draw 2 shapes: a small oval at the lower left center of the grid, and then a rounded "balloon" shape starting from the right of the small oval toward the center of the grid.

2.

On the right of the balloon shape, draw curved lines to form the tail.

Next, draw a short set of front legs and a large set of rear legs, each with 3 toes.

3.

In the small oval, draw the head detail.

Following the upper curve of the body and tail, draw a series of small to large triangular plates that end at the tail in 2 long, pointy spikes.

4. Draw in the nostril, dot for the eye, mouth line, and small curves to separate the claws from the feet.

Finally, draw upside-down V-shaped lines to show the triangular plates on the other side of the dino.

5. Ink the dinosaur and erase the grid.
Color the dino's body GREEN on top and YELLOW on the bottom.

Make the triangular plates a REDDISH-BROWN color.

Triceratops

Along with the T-Rex, triceratops is one of the most famous of all dinosaurs. With its armored plating, it looks like a distant cousin to the rhinoceros. It had three horns on its face and a parrot-like beak for a mouth. Triceratops may look formidable and fierce, but it was, in fact, a plant-eater living in great herds for protection. The four short legs meant that triceratops was slow-moving. It was a favorite food for T-Rex. Fossils were first discovered in Colorado in 1888 and have since been found in other sites in western Canada and the United States.

1. Draw a grid with 4 squares going across and 3 down.

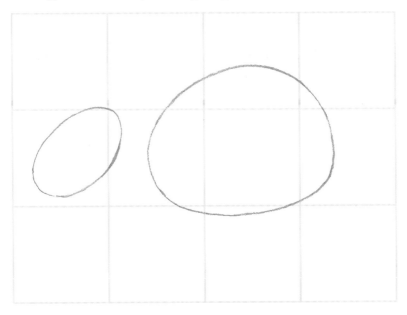

Draw 2 ovals: a large one to the right center of the grid, and then a smaller, egg-shaped one to the left center of the grid.

2.

Draw the curved lines of the neck to connect the 2 ovals.

Next, draw the curved lines for the tail.

Then draw the shapes for the legs.

3. On the egg-shaped oval, draw in the lines of the face. Make the mouth beak-like, like a parrot's.

Now draw in the large plate for the back of the head.

4.

Draw in the nostril and eyeball.

Now we'll draw the horns: 1 on the snout, 2 jutting out from just above the eye, and 1 on the "cheek."

Draw in the toe claws and toes on the dino's feet.

5.

Ink your drawing and erase the grid.
Color the dino a GREENISH-YELLOW with a PALE ORANGE underside. Color the horns WHITE.

Compsognathus

About the size of a modern-day chicken, compsognathus (the name means "pretty jaw") is one of the smallest known dinosaurs. It was speedy and quite agile, getting around on two pencil-thin legs capped by three-toed feet.

Its small, pointed head sitting on a long, flexible neck featured a large mouth with an array of tiny but sharp teeth. Its two short arms helped it catch its diet of small animals and insects. A fossil was first discovered in the late 1850s in southern Germany. Later, a second fossil was excavated in France. To date, that's all that's been found.

1. Draw a grid with 4 squares going across and 3 down.

Draw two oval shapes: one to the left-center of the grid, the other smaller in the top-left corner of the grid.

2. Connect the two shapes by drawing two curved lines between them to form the neck of the dino.

On the far right of the center oval, draw 2 curved lines for a long tail.

3. Draw in the shape of the two 2 arms.

Next, draw in the shape of the 2 long legs.
Spread the legs apart to show that the dino is walking.

4. To finish the drawing, draw in the long mouth and round eyeball.

Then draw 2 curved claws for hands and draw in the 3-clawed feet. Add an additional claw to each foot on the heels of the dino.

5. Ink your dino and erase the grid and pencil lines.

Color the dino a PALE TANNISH color. Add some DEEP BLUE color to the top of the head and wavy BLUE lines to the dino's upper body.

Ankylosaurus

This huge (35 foot/11m long), fierce-looking, armored dinosaur was, in all probability, a big, gentle, not-too-bright plant-eater. It was covered in thick, bony plates and two rows of sharp spikes that offered ample protection from predators. If this weren't enough, its club-like tail could be a formidable weapon. Only its underbelly was vulnerable. In spite of its short legs, it was capable of running at a good clip. Fossils were first found in 1908 and have been recovered in Montana and Alberta, Canada. Tracks (which help determine the speed at which a dinosaur moved) have been found in Bolivia, South America.

1. Draw a grid with 3 squares going across and 3 down.

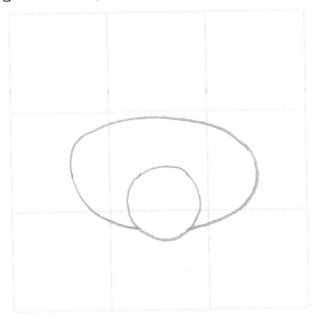

Draw 2 shapes in the center of the grid. One shape will be a circle, the other will be an oval drawn around the circle.

2.

On both side of the oval shape, draw 4 legs.

On the circle, draw a wide "V" for the mouth and 2 small circles for eyes.

Above the oval body, draw a circle with 2 curved lines under it.

3.

Add a series of upside-down "V" shapes along the top of the oval body shape, following the curve of the oval. Make 4 more rows of these toward the head shape.

Next, add 3 curved lines inside the circle that you drew above the body.

Now, add 4 more v-shaped spikes on both sides of the dino's head.

4.

Add some more rows of smaller spikes to the tail of the dino.

Draw small, straight lines down the centers of all the spikes.

Add the toes and claws to the feet.

Last, add 2 circular nostrils in the middle of the head toward the mouth, and add 2 dots in the eyes.

5.

Ink your dino and erase the grid.

Color the dino a DARK TAN.

Color the spikes a LIGHT TAN.

Shade the spikes light on one side and dark on the other to make them more real!

Pteranodon

Not a dinosaur, but a flying reptile, pteranodon had a wingspread of up to 33 feet (10m), wider than any known bird's. If it stood on its two legs, it would reach a height of 6 feet (2m). Brainy—that is to say, they had large brains—with excellent eyesight, pteranodons were carnivores even though they had no teeth. Some scientists believe they ate like pelicans, scooping their prey from the water and swallowing them whole. Fossils have been known since 1876 and have been found primarily in Kansas and England.

1. Draw a grid with 4 squares going across and 3 down.

Draw 2 shapes in the center of the grid.

Draw the larger shape toward the left of the center of the grid. Start by drawing the letter "W," and extend two lines upward to a point.

To the right of the 1st shape, draw a sideways "tear" shape.

2.

Next, draw 2 arms with 3 pointy fingers stretched in a "V" shape between the first 2 shapes.

Next, on the pointy end of the "tear" shape, draw 2 clawed feet.

3.

Draw the wings of the dino and connect the bottom of the right wing to the right foot.

4.

Last, draw in the round eyeball sockets and mouth lines.

5. Ink the drawing and erase the grid.

Color the dino BRIGHT ORANGE and
the inside of the wings an
ORANGE-YELLOW.

Dilong paradoxus

Newly discovered fossils in 2004 in northeastern China gave us our first glimpse of dilong paradoxus, a small feathered dinosaur that was a primitive relative of the gigantic T-Rex. These feathers were clearly for warmth, not flying, and many scientists are exploring the possibility that even large dinosaurs had feathers at some stage in their development, perhaps losing them as they matured. Many dinosaurs share characteristics of modern-day birds and, like birds, may have been warm-blooded, unlike cold-blooded reptiles. Dilong was 5 feet long (1.6m) and, like the T-Rex, a meat-eater.

1. Draw a grid with 2 squares going across and 4 down.

Draw 2 oval-like shapes, one in the upper left corner of the grid, and another, larger one in the center of the grid.

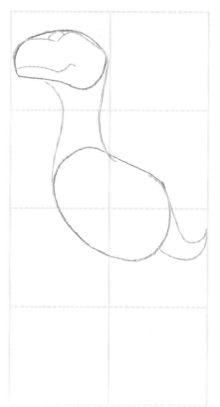

2.

Next, connect the 2 ovals using 2 curved lines.

Then do another set of curved lines that form a curved point on the right of the center of the oval.

Draw in the mouth lines and 2 rounded bumps on the top of the head.

Add a curve for the snout.

3.

Draw in the arms and legs. Make sure to start them in the center of the body oval.

Give this dino 3 large, pointy fingers.

4.

Add some "zig-zag" strokes to chow that thic dino ic furry. Draw these on the back of the dino's neck toward his head and on top of the dino's tail.

> Draw the curves on the hands and feet to separate the claws.

> Add an additional claw on the back of the dino's left foot.

5.

Ink the dino with your pen and erase the grid.

> Color the dino's head, hands and feet PINK.

> Color the dino's fur a DARK BLUISH-GREEN to a BRIGHT YELLOW to a BRIGHT ORANGE at the top.

Hagryphus giganteus

In 2005, scientists digging in southern Utah found the fossilized hands and feet of what turned out to be the remains of a new and rather bizarre feathered dinosaur. Named for the Egyptian god of the western desert (Ha) and a Greek mythological bird (griffin), hagryphus was an enormous, birdlike creature (10 feet/ 3m long, 7 feet/2m tall) that looked like a giant, technicolor turkey. Hagryphus had a toothless beak but strong arms and claws that allowed it to eat both meat and plants.

1. Draw a grid with 4 squares going across and 4 down.

Draw 3 shapes: a circle in the middle of the grid, an oval in the upper right of the grid, and a curved "fan" shape in the upper left of the grid.

2.

Connect the fan shape to the center circle using 2 curved lines.

Connect the oval to the center circle by making 2 wide, curved lines.

Draw in the arms and a curved "W" shape for the top of the legs.

Give this dino 2 rounded fingers.

3. Now, within the fan shape, add some long, wavy lines.

Add a row of feathers to the bottom of each arm.

Draw a series of curves within the head shape and add a slanted, rectangular shape to the top of the head.

Then, finish drawing the legs and feet.

4.

Add some "zig-zag" fur lines to the dino.

Add the details of the head, including the eyes, pointy tongue, and nostril.

Now draw in the claws on the hands and feet.

Add a 4th claw to the back of the longer leg.

5.

Ink your drawing and erase the grid.

Color the dino's body REDDISH-BROWN, but the make the underside of the dino a GRAYISH-WHITE.

Make the head and underarm feathers BLUE.

The hands, feet, beak, and rectangle shape above the head should be YELLOW.

The fan shape at the end of the tail can be BROWN to WHITE to BLUE.

Guanlong wucaii

Early in 2006, scientists announced that fossils belonging to the oldest (to date) relative of the T-Rex had been discovered. Named guanlong wucaii, this creature had a spectacular, multi-colored crest on its head. The crest is a bit of a mystery, since it is too fragile to use for defense. Guanlong was about the size of a T-Rex. It was feathered like a chicken and a meat-eater with long, sharp teeth. Its two long, powerful back legs would have allowed it to race about swiftly. Its two shorter arms were capped by three fingers and long nails that were ideal for slicing and dicing.

1. Draw a grid with 4 squares going across and 3 down.

Draw 2 egg-shaped ovals: one in the upper center of the grid and another, slightly smaller one at an angle toward the upper left corner of the grid.

2.

Draw a series of curved lines, 1 set for the neck, and another set to form the tail.

Draw an oval shape at the end of the tail shape.

Next, draw the curved lines for the arms and legs and round out the toes and fingers.

3.

Draw the mouth and lower head-shape lines.

Add an angled, oval shape to the head just above the mouth.

Last, add "wavy" feather lines to the neck, under the arms, and around the oval shape at the end of the tail.

4. Now to finish the drawing. Add 2 rows of tiny, pointed teeth.

Draw in the nostril and eyeball. Also add a curved line in the oval shape that you drew on top of the head.

Draw in the last leg and some pointy, triangle-shaped fingernails and toenails.

5. Color the dino a PINKISH TAN.

Add a large, PURPLE patch to the back of the dino.

Make the oval shape on the head a BRIGHT PINK.

Color the feathers under the arms a GRAYISH PURPLE.

Use many long strokes to give the dino the "feathered" look!

Incisivosaurus gauthieri

Fossils belonging to one of the oddest-looking dinosaurs ever were found in northeast China in 2002. Incisivosaurus was about the size of a turkey, feathered and fast. It looked like a cross between the extinct dodo bird and a rabbit. The rodent-like, protruding front teeth probably meant that incisivosaurus was content to gnaw on plants, seeds and vegetables rather than meat. Like many modern birds, it swallowed pebbles to help grind up its food.

1.

Draw a grid with 3 squares going across and 4 down.

Then draw 2 circles: one toward the left center of the grid, and one slightly smaller one toward the top-right corner of the grid.

2.

Next, draw a whole bunch of curved lines to make the neck, tail, arms, legs, and mouth, plus a circle for the eye of our dino.

Give the arms and legs 3 pointy fingers and toes each, and draw the tail pointing upwards.

3.

Now add the wavy lines to give our dino feathers!

Add them to the back of the arms, down the neck, and on top of the body.

Also, add feathers to the top of the neck, ending at the top of the head.

Lastly, add a flame-like feather shape above the tail!

44

4.

Define the bumpy shape of the head and add an eyeball and nostril dot.

Add ring shapes to separate the fingernails from the hands and small curves to separate the toenails from the feet.

Draw in the curve of the mouth and give this dino 2 big "buckteeth."

5.

Ink the dino and erase the grid.

Color the body a TANNISH GRAY.

Color the face and feet YELLOW.

Color the feathers behind the arms and on the tail a DEEP BLUE.

Erketu Ellisoni

Imagine putting a 24 foot (7m)-long neck on a school bus and adding a 12 foot (4m)-long tail. This would give you an idea of the size of an erketu ellisoni, which was actually a modest-sized sauropod. Sauropods were semi-aquatic, four-legged, plant-eating dinosaurs with incredibly long necks that were among the largest living creatures ever. Erketu, like other sauropods, probably strolled with its head and neck parallel to the ground. Still, it's hard to imagine how they walked without falling on their faces. Erketu fossils were first found in 2002 in the Gobi Desert of Mongolia.

1. Draw a grid with 4 squares going across and 2 down.

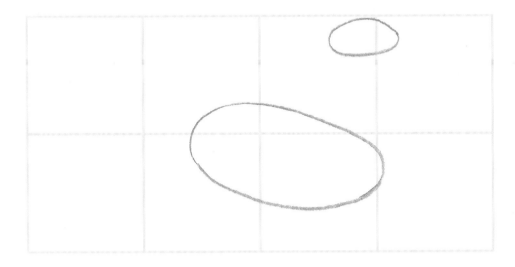

Draw 2 ovals: one large one in the center of the grid, and one smaller one at the top of the grid toward the right of the first oval.

2. Draw 2 lines to the left of the large oval and have them curve downward and meet at a point.

Next, draw 2 more lines that curve toward the head oval, then draw the dip of the head.

3. On the large oval, draw in the legs and feet, which are shaped sort of like thick chicken drumsticks.

4. On the feet, draw tiny curves to make toes.

On the head, add an eye, mouth and dot for the nostril.

Last, add a curved "neck-bend" line at the middle of the long neck.

5. Ink the dino and erase the grid.

Color the dino a GRASSY GREEN!